W9-ACF-073

CLASSIC
StoryTellers

NATHANIEL HAWTHORNE

Mitchell Lane
PUBLISHERS

P.O. Box 196
Hockessin, Delaware 19707

Titles in the Series

Judy Blume

Ray Bradbury

Beverly Cleary

Stephen Crane

F. Scott Fitzgerald

Nathaniel Hawthorne

Ernest Hemingway

Jack London

Katherine Paterson

Edgar Allan Poe

John Steinbeck

Harriet Beecher Stowe

Mildred Taylor

Mark Twain

E. B. White

CLASSIC
StoryTellers

NATHANIEL HAWTHORNE

Russell Roberts

Mitchell Lane
PUBLISHERS

Printing   1   2   3   4   5   6   7   8   9

Library of Congress Cataloging-in-Publication Data
Roberts, Russell, 1953–
        Nathaniel Hawthorne / by Russell Roberts.
              p. cm — (Classic storytellers)
        Includes bibliographical references and index.
        ISBN 1-58415-454-3 (library bound)
    1. Hawthorne, Nathaniel, 1804-1864—Juvenile literature. 2. Novelists, American—19th century —Biography—Juvenile literature. I. Title. II. Series.
PS1881.R63 2006
813'.3—dc22
                                                                        2005027983
ISBN–10: 1-58415-454-3   ISBN–13: 987-1-58415-454-9

ABOUT THE AUTHOR: Russell Roberts has written and published over 35 books for adults and children on a variety of subjects, including baseball, memory power, business, New Jersey history, and travel. He has also written numerous books for Mitchell Lane, including *Pedro Menendez de Aviles, Philo Farnsworth Invents TV, Robert Goddard, Bernardo de Galvez,* and *Where Did All the Dinosaurs Go?* He lives in Bordentown, New Jersey, with his family and a fat, fuzzy, and crafty calico cat named Rusti.

PHOTO CREDITS: Cover, pp. 1, 3, 6, 10 Library of Congress; p. 16 Corbis; pp. 19, 21 Library of Congress; p. 24 Associated Press/Lisa Poole; pp. 28, 32, 34, 36, 41 Library of Congress

PUBLISHER'S NOTE: This story is based on the author's extensive research, which he believes to be accurate. Documentation of such research is contained on page 46.
        The internet sites referenced herein were active as of the publication date. Due to the fleeting nature of some web sites, we cannot guarantee they will all be active when you are reading this book.

                                                                        PLB

Contents

NATHANIEL HAWTHORNE

Russell Roberts

*For Your Information

StoryTellers StoryTellers StoryTellers StoryTellers StoryTellers StoryTellers

George Burroughs during the Salem Witch Trials. Burroughs was considered by many to be the ringleader of the witches. Arrested while eating dinner, he was convicted of witchcraft, despite pleas of innocence by his friends, and hanged.

Chapter 1

FINANCIAL WORRIES

Forty-one-year-old Nathaniel Hawthorne sat at his desk in his bedroom, his chin in his hand. His steel gray eyes stared into space. His fingers drummed nervously.

In front of him were a quill pen and some blank sheets of paper. Every so often he'd dip his pen into the inkwell and write some words or a few sentences on the paper. Then, more often than not, he'd cross out many of the words he had just written.

Occasionally he'd get up and walk over to one of the room's windows, hands behind his back. The New England winter had stripped the trees of all their leaves. Hawthorne stared at the bare brown limbs for a long time, then turned and walked slowly back to his desk. Sighing, he sat down, picked up his pen, and dipped it into the ink again. The tip hovered over the piece of paper. A small dot of ink dripped from the pen. Finally he put the pen down, shaking his head. The words just would not come.

He had already published numerous short stories and some story collections. The reviews had been very good. He was being called a great writer. But few people were buying his works, and he was getting paid very little for his stories. He and his family—wife Sophia and daughter Una—had been forced to leave their home in Concord, Massachusetts, because they had not paid the rent. With nowhere else to go, Hawthorne and his family had moved into his mother's house in Salem, Massachusetts.

Salem was the town in which he had grown up. It was famous for two things: the sea and witches. Salem had a long history of ships and sailing. Many people who lived there made their living from the sea. It was also the site of the Salem Witch Trials in 1692. Twenty innocent people thought to be witches had been executed. One of Hawthorne's ancestors, John Hathorne, had been a magistrate of the court that convicted them.

Hawthorne had come home again . . . but it was not a very happy homecoming. He was returning as a destitute failure, a man who could not support his family. He took over his old bedroom, the one in which he used to dream about being a writer. Those dreams seemed hollow now.

To create even more concern, Sophia was pregnant. How could he afford a new baby? He desperately hoped that his friends in politics would get him a job. That would solve all his problems—a steady job with a steady salary. But day after day passed, and he didn't hear a word. No job. No money. Nothing.

He again picked up his pen and dipped it into the ink, but after a moment he put it back down. He ran his fingers through his dark hair. What was he going to do? What was he going to do?

The above is a portrait of Nathaniel Hawthorne in the early winter of 1846. We don't know if everything just described really happened, but the portrait is based on actual events. Having been put out of their home because they hadn't paid the rent, the Hawthornes had moved back in with Nathaniel's mother. His wife, Sophia, was pregnant with their second child. We know that he could not write when his mind was troubled. We also know that he was broke and was worried about what he was going to do if the new baby arrived before he got a job. Hawthorne was destitute, depressed, and worried.

That winter was the lowest point of Hawthorne's life. Little did he realize what the future held. . . .

FYInfo

Salem Witch Trials

Salem, Massachusetts, the town in which Nathaniel Hawthorne was born and lived at various times, will forever be remembered in history for its infamous witch trials. These notorious proceedings resulted in the deaths of twenty innocent men and women.

The witch hysteria began in the summer of 1692 when several young girls began acting mysteriously. Failing to "cure" them, a doctor suggested that their illnesses may have been super-natural in origin. Suspicion fell on Tituba, a slave who had been telling the girls about voodoo and magic. To save herself, she admitted to being in league with Satan. The girls began accusing other people of being witches. They would fall to the ground, scream, and twitch uncontrollably when they saw the people. Supposedly the people's specter (invisible image) was tormenting them.

When the people accused as witches were brought to trial, the girls would go into their act. It was later determined that those accused of witchcraft were unpopular townspeople whom the girls had simply singled out. It was a time of extreme nervousness for everyone in Salem and the surrounding area. All it took to be labeled a witch was to be accused by the girls, and no one knew whom they would go after next. Nineteen people were hanged as witches, and one man was pressed to death by heavy rocks. Many more people, including children, were left to rot in jail.

Eventually Salem realized its mistake and the madness stopped. A few years later one judge in the witch trials, Samuel Sewall, publicly admitted his error, but it was far too late for all those condemned to die. Since then, Salem has forever been known as the Witch Town. The modern town of Salem has built a thriving tourist trade on the infamous events of that time.

For many years, most of Salem's residents depended on the sea to make a living. But life at sea was dangerous and uncertain. One day Nathaniel Hawthorne's father set sail from Salem and never returned.

Chapter 2

THE BOY WHO WANTED TO BE A WRITER

Nathaniel Hathorne (he later changed his name to Hawthorne) never really knew his father. Captain Nathaniel Hathorne loved the sea as much as he loved his wife, Elizabeth. He was always on a voyage to some far and distant land. Young Nathaniel hardly ever saw him.

But the boy did read his father's journals, which were filled with information about life at sea. The books fired his imagination. The sea sounded romantic, exciting, and full of adventure.

Captain Hathorne was often gone for long stretches from the house on Union Street in Salem, where the Hathornes lived. He was at sea when his first child, Nathaniel's sister Elizabeth (nicknamed Ebe), was born on March 7, 1802. Two years later, on July 4, 1804, he was at sea again when Nathaniel was born.

In December 1807, Captain Hathorne once again headed out to sea. On January 9, 1808, Nathaniel's second sister, Maria Louisa (called Louisa), was born. Shortly thereafter, still out at sea, Captain Hathorne caught yellow fever. At the time, no one knew what caused this horrible disease, and no one knew how to cure it. Captain Hathorne died.

He left his wife an estate of just $296.21. Devastated emotionally and financially, Elizabeth and her three young children moved in with her parents, Richard and Miriam Manning, who lived on Herbert Street in Salem. The Mannings' house was lively and crowded. Already living there were their eight other children, a great-aunt, a servant, and several cats. Nathaniel added to the menagerie for a time by having a pet monkey.

Although he knew the sea was dangerous, Nathaniel initially wanted to be a sailor. Supposedly his earliest writings were about sailors, ships, and pirates.

In April 1813, Nathaniel's grandfather Manning died. His twenty-four-year-old uncle Robert became Nathaniel's third "father."

That summer, when he was nine, Nathaniel hurt his foot at school. He had to use crutches for over a year. Because of the injury, he did not go to school. Instead, his teacher, Joseph Worcester, came to his home.

The foot injury turned out to be a blessing in disguise. Unable to play army with his friends, Nathaniel read instead. He usually read lying on the carpet at home, surrounded by books (he even made a house of books for the cats).

In the winter of 1815, Elizabeth Hathorne announced that she and her children were going to the Manning family's property on the banks of the Sebago Lake in Raymond, Maine, to live. Nathaniel's foot injury suddenly got better.

After several postponements and short trips to Raymond, the Hathornes finally arrived in Maine for an extended period in the autumn of 1818. The three children were very happy there, especially Nathaniel. He tracked bears in the woods, fished in the ponds and streams, and explored.

"I ran quite wild . . . fishing all day long, or shooting with an old fowling-piece; but reading a good deal too,"[1] Hawthorne remembered.

Although he stayed in Maine less than a year, the lifestyle there helped Nathaniel grow tall and strong. He became a good shot and an even better fisherman. The woods and the people he met stimulated his imagination.

But Uncle Robert insisted that Nathaniel go to school. Nathaniel hated school and tried to attend as little as possible, but he could not ignore his uncle's wishes. In the winter of 1818 he attended a boarding school just outside Portland, Maine. Unhappy, he threatened to run away. He was returned to Salem and went to school there. He attended dancing classes, learned to swim, and played badminton. But nothing could replace the town of Raymond.

"I shall never again run wild in Raymond, and I shall never be so happy as when I did,"[2] Hawthorne said with regret.

Missing Raymond, and not feeling comfortable in Salem, where he had problems with both his aunt Mary and his grandmother, Nathaniel tried to bring both worlds together in a family newspaper he wrote called *The Spectator.* It recorded the activities of his family in both places.

Over the next few years Nathaniel Hathorne tried to find a career. He considered law, medicine, and religion, but rejected all of them. Being a writer interested him, but he had one major concern—it was difficult to make a living as an author. "[A]uthors are always poor Devils, and therefore Satan may take them,"[3] he said. Still, he spent much time in his room under the eaves, writing stories.

In the autumn of 1821, he entered Bowdoin College in Brunswick, Maine. He enjoyed college life more than he thought, because in addition to studying, he drank, smoked, gambled, and cut class—all of which were against the rules. He helped found two drinking clubs, the Pot-8-O Club and the Androscoggin Club. One of his classmates and friends at Bowdoin was Franklin Pierce, who would eventually become the fourteenth president of the United States. Another was the future famous poet Henry Wadsworth Longfellow.

As a young man, Hathorne was muscular and handsome, with dark wavy hair and thick eyebrows. He was apparently so good-looking that an elderly woman once stopped him in the street and wanted to know if she was addressing a man or an angel. When he walked, he swung his right arm and tilted his head a bit to the left, as if he were trying to keep his balance while walking on a ship. He was quiet and shy around people he didn't know, but more talkative around his friends.

Still, all the fun that he had at school could not sweep away his increasingly gloomy disposition. "I am tired of college . . . and . . . I am heartily tired of myself,"⁴ he said.

On September 7, 1825, Hathorne graduated college 18th in a class of nearly 40. However, his poor attendance record disqualified him from speaking at the graduation ceremony. After graduation he returned to Salem, still uncertain what to do with his life.

While at college he had written stories. Once he was back in Salem, he stayed in his room under the eaves most of the day, writing and revising them. In pleasant weather he went out for an afternoon walk. Sometimes he'd hike along the beach, watching the water sweep over the rocks and then retreat again. He stayed to himself so much that he didn't feel there were twenty people in Salem who knew him.

Hathorne would often use the old wills and other papers located in Salem for research. His fertile imagination developed characters, plots, and atmosphere from this material. If he did not use it right away, he stored the information away for the future. Salem's rich history with both the sea and the witch trials provided him with a gold mine of material. He also used some of the Maine legends he had heard. Supposedly he did not like to gather material himself. Instead he sent out Ebe, who returned with reading material for him.

When it came to his writing, Hathorne was his own worst critic. All through his entire writing career, he was impatient with and demanding of himself. He became frustrated when something was not as good as he thought it should be. He would burn writing that did not get published. In the mid-1820s, he tried to publish a collection of his stories called *Seven Tales of My Native Land*. When it was rejected, he burned it.

But he did not give up.

FYInfo

Henry Wadsworth Longfellow

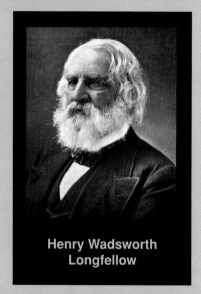

Henry Wadsworth Longfellow

Henry Wadsworth Longfellow, a classmate of Hawthorne's at Bowdoin College, became one of America's most beloved poets and writers.

Born in Portland, Maine (which was then a part of Massachusetts), Longfellow taught first at Bowdoin, and then at Harvard. His first volume of poetry was *Voices in the Night,* published in 1839. It established his reputation as one of the great American poets for its simplicity of language and familiar themes. In 1854 he retired from teaching and devoted himself exclusively to writing.

Longfellow's poetry was immensely popular. He had a natural ability to create simple but memorable rhymes. This enabled people to easily remember and quote from his poems. He also wrote about American themes and traditions. This gave Americans a natural pride in reading his work.

In 1861 he was devastated when his second wife was burned to death in a household accident. In 1863 he published *Tales of a Wayside Inn.* It contains one of his most famous poems, "Paul Revere's Ride." Among his other memorable poems are *The Song of Hiawatha* (1855) and *The Courtship of Miles Standish* (1858).

The popularity of his poetry is often given credit for establishing an audience for poetry in the United States. For instance, his 1841 poem "The Village Blacksmith" makes mention of a chestnut tree. When the actual chestnut tree that he had written about had to be taken down, children donated their pennies to turn the tree into a chair, which was given to Longfellow.

Longfellow died on March 24, 1882. In 1884, his bust was placed in the Poet's Corner of London's Westminster Abbey. He was the first American to be so honored.

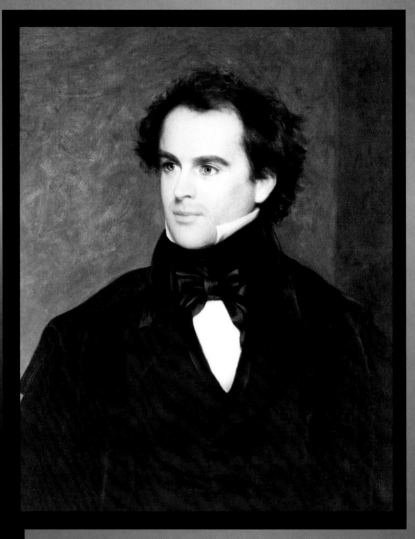

Famous portrait artist Charles Osgood made this painting of Nathaniel Hawthorne in 1840. By this time, Hawthorne was secretly engaged to be married.

Chapter 3

A NEW NAME AND
A NEW LOVE

Around 1825 Hathorne had practiced writing his name by adding the letter *w* after the *a:* Hawthorne. Two years later he used the new spelling again. Soon he was using it consistently. Eventually his sisters used the new spelling too.

Why did he change the spelling of his name? No one knows for sure. One guess is that he did not want to be thought of as a Hathorne. Once, right after he changed the spelling, somebody said to him that he didn't look like a Hathorne from Salem.

"I am glad to hear you say that," he replied, "for I don't wish to look like any Hathorne."[1]

Although he changed his name, he published his first novel anonymously in 1828. Called *Fanshawe: A Tale,* it was about college life, romance, greed, and death. He probably paid the Boston publishers Marsh and Capen $100 to print it. (At this time in America, writers usually paid to have their books printed.) But eventually his inner critic emerged. He destroyed every copy of *Fanshawe* he could find, including his sister's.

Even though Hawthorne was actively writing, he was still uncertain about his future. He was anxious to figure out a path for his life. Although he was handsome, he wasn't interested in courting women. Still a loner, he did not go out much in the evening. He'd stay in, eating a pint bowl of chocolate mixed with crumbled bread. In the summer he'd substitute fruit for the chocolate.

In the spring of 1829, Hawthorne, still writing, mailed a few stories to Samuel Griswold Goodrich, an editor and author who wanted to publish American writers. Impressed, Goodrich offered to find a publisher for a new set of Hawthorne's stories titled *Provincial Tales of My Native Land.*

Goodrich also wanted Hawthorne's stories for *The Token,* a book of stories that appeared just before Christmas each year. Ten Hawthorne stories appeared in the 1831, 1832, and 1833 editions. The stories that appeared were anonymous, as were his stories that appeared in the *Salem Gazette.* Publishing anonymously was the custom at the time.

In the summer of 1831, Hawthorne journeyed through New Hampshire with another uncle, Samuel. The following summer he visited Vermont, Niagara Falls, and a few other places.

He often traveled throughout New England over the next few years. His observations of people, places, and events became material for his stories. He recorded his observations in his notebooks, which he filled with ideas for plots, descriptions of people, details about places, and anything else he thought might someday make a good story.

His travels in 1831 gave Hawthorne the idea for a book of stories called *The Story Teller.* It was a two-volume collection of stories based on the lighthearted adventures of a wandering author. Goodrich rejected it. Instead, he took a few stories out of it. The rest of the manuscript passed to *New-England Magazine,* which printed a few more stories. The stories were never printed all together, as Hawthorne had inteded.

Hawthorne's uncle Samuel died on November 17, 1833. His death depressed Hawthorne, as did his anonymous writing career. He bitterly thought himself "the obscurest [most unknown] man of letters in America."[2] A solitary man to begin with, Hawthorne withdrew even further, spending much time in his room. The culture of New England was infused with the idea that work was manual labor. Hawthorne felt guilty that he was not working a "regular" job. He continued to live in Salem in a household dominated by women: his two sisters, his mother,

Hawthorne would hold several jobs in the city of Boston, viewed here from Dorchester Heights around 1840.

and his aunt Mary. The old days, when the house brimmed with life, must have seemed very distant indeed.

In January 1836, Hawthorne took a job in Boston editing a monthly magazine called the *American Magazine of Useful and Entertaining Knowledge,* published by the Berwick Company. The salary would be $500 per year.

Hawthorne's job as editor was to find whatever information he could and write short articles about it for the magazine. He wrote about anything and everything, from New England farmers to noses to George Washington. Except for a few contributions by his sister Ebe back in Salem, he was the magazine's sole writer.

Since each issue of the magazine contained as many as forty articles, Hawthorne was constantly searching for new material. His job was made more difficult when the company would not pay for him to use Boston's private library.

In fact, Berwick did not even pay him his salary. Hawthorne was so poor that he couldn't afford to pay nine cents for a glass of wine and a cigar. "For the Devil's sake, if you have money, send me a little," he begged his sister Louisa. "It is now a month since I left Salem, and not a damned cent have I had, except five dollars that I borrowed of Uncle Robert—and out of that I paid my stage fare and other expenses."[3]

In June the Berwick Company went bankrupt, having paid Hawthorne only $20 of his salary. Back in Salem and depressed, he contemplated his life: Hawthorne was an unknown and financially destitute author, while some of his Bowdoin classmates, such as Pierce (Speaker of the House of Representatives) and Longfellow (Harvard College instructor and poet) were doing far better. Little did he know that the "unknown" part, at least, was about to change. Both his friend Horatio Bridge and Park Benjamin of the magazine *American Monthly* announced in print in the fall of 1836 that Hawthorne was the anonymous author of some of the best American stories published.

"[O]f the few American writers by profession, one of the very best is a gentleman whose name has never yet been made public . . . ," wrote Bridge. "We refer to Nathaniel Hawthorne, Esq., of Salem."[4] Benjamin was equally complimentary, saying that Hawthorne would be successful if he collected his stories into one volume.

Taking Benjamin's advice, Hawthorne collected eighteen of his stories for publication. Because all had been previously published, he called the collection *Twice-Told Tales*. Bridge paid for the book's publication in March 1837. Reviews were positive. However, although it sold well, it was not a financial success for Hawthorne, and he continued to scrape for money. Pierce, a U.S. Senator, tried to get him an appointment as an historian on an expedition to the South Seas, raising Hawthorne's hopes that he would finally get to go to sea. Pierce was unsuccessful.

Once again, Hawthorne contemplated his life and decided that all he had done was stay in his room writing stories while life passed him by. "I have made a captive of myself and put me into a dungeon," he said, "and now I cannot find the key to let myself out."[5]

Hawthorne seems to have enjoyed his job at the Boston Custom House. It also kept him close to Sophia Peabody.

The person who held the key was a small woman with chestnut brown hair and large blue eyes named Sophia Peabody. She was a semi-invalid, suffering from bad headaches, sleeplessness, and constant fatigue. Loud noises bothered her; the clatter of silverware at dinnertime sent her running up to her bedroom. She was also an artist; during her long stretches alone in her room she drew pictures, then displayed them as if her bedroom were an art gallery.

Initially, Hawthorne and his sister Ebe came to the Peabody home in the autumn of 1837 because of Sophia's sister Elizabeth. At first, Sophia shyly hid behind her bedroom door, but soon she was coming down when he came over, laughing and talking with him. When Elizabeth went out of town to help set up a school, Sophia and Nathaniel became closer.

Chapter 3   A NEW NAME AND A NEW LOVE

In July 1838 Hawthorne left Salem for another of his journeys. He told Sophia that he planned to change his name so if he should die, no one could find his grave. Upon his return to Salem that autumn, Nathaniel and Sophia continued their romance. Then Sophia left for a few weeks to study sculpture and stay with friends in Boston. In early January 1839, Hawthorne was appointed measurer of coal and salt at the Boston Custom House. The salary was $1,500 per year. While the job was not great, it gave him an excuse to be in Boston at the same time as Sophia. The two grew closer and closer until they decided to become engaged.

Both wanted to keep their relationship secret. When Sophia returned to Salem, Hawthorne remained in Boston at his job, and they saw each other infrequently. The distance between them helped to keep their romance quiet. They also went through elaborate deceptions to keep their secret. His letters to her were carefully timed to arrive every other Saturday, as if from a casual friend. She disguised her handwriting in letters to him, sending them to the Custom House, so that no one would know he was getting letters from a woman.

Hawthorne may have felt that taking the job at the Custom House would give him plenty of opportunity to write, but that was not the case. He said that he couldn't write because he no longer felt in control of his time. In reality, he actually liked his job. He'd walk over to the ships docked at the wharves to weigh and measure cargoes of coal. As he worked he smoked a cigar, talked to the sailors, or watched other ships as they came in and out of Boston Harbor, wondering where they had been or where they were going. His old love of the sea had returned.

"It was exhilarating to see the vessels, how they bounded over the waves, while a sheet of foam broke out around them,"[6] he told Sophia.

He must have also been pleased at the money he was making. He earned extra fees for measuring salt and coal. For a man accustomed to scraping for cash, the sudden appearance of it must have been exciting.

Through the spring of 1840, Hawthorne and Sophia continued their secret engagement. As it continued with no end in sight, even Sophia grew tired of it.

Little did she realize how much longer it would go on.

FYInfo

Elizabeth Peabody

Nathaniel Hawthorne's sister-in-law Elizabeth Peabody became just as famous as Hawthorne in some respects.

Born on May 16, 1804, Elizabeth was educated by her mother. It was an era in which a woman's education was not considered important or necessary. She showed interest in philosophy and religious issues at an early age. As a young woman she opened several schools, and she also studied Greek with young Ralph Waldo Emerson.

Peabody felt that she had "discovered" Hawthorne. While that is not entirely true, she did admire the stories he had written anonymously in *The Token,* and set out to discover the identity of the writer. (When she found out that the writer was a Hawthorne, she wrongly assumed that the writer was his sister Ebe, whom she remembered from childhood.) Indeed, Peabody can be considered responsible for Hawthorne's meeting his wife, for if it were not for Elizabeth's invitation to her home to meet him, he would perhaps never have met Sophia.

Her exact relationship with Hawthorne is something that will never be known. Some think they were romantically involved; others, that they were just good friends. Certainly she gave Hawthorne a much-needed boost

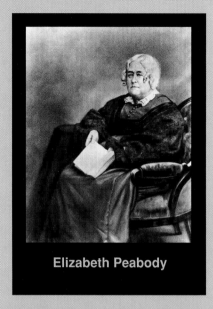

Elizabeth Peabody

of confidence in his writing, for which he was forever grateful.

After her schools closed, Elizabeth Peabody supported herself by writing and private tutoring. In 1837 she became a charter member of the Transcendentalist Club, along with Emerson, Margaret Fuller, and other great thinkers of the time. On her own printing press she published books by Fuller and Hawthorne, and she is credited as being the first female book publisher in America.

Around 1860 she learned of the German educational class known as kindergarten. The following year she opened the first formal kindergarten in the United States in Boston. Much of her later writing dealt with education and kindergarten. She died on January 3, 1894.

The famous House of the Seven Gables in Salem, Massachusetts. It is this house in which Hawthorne set one of his most famous stories. The house is open for tours, and visitors can walk through it and try to imagine how Hawthorne experienced it.

Chapter 4

DESPERATION AND TRIUMPH

In July 1840, Elizabeth Peabody opened a circulating library and bookshop in Boston. It became a meeting place for followers of a new philosophy, transcendentalism. This philosophy proposed that every person's soul had divine possibilities. Among the members of this group were Ralph Waldo Emerson and Margaret Fuller, a champion of women's rights. Sophia embraced transcendentalism, but Hawthorne did not. He had a darker view of humanity, believing that people were corrupt and that the human heart was a dark and dreary place.

When William Henry Harrison was elected president, Hawthorne resigned his job rather than serve under him. By March he had produced three history books for children called *The Whole History of Grandfather's Chair, Famous Old People,* and *The Liberty Tree.* Elizabeth Peabody published all three. Unfortunately, they did not sell very well.

Hawthorne also talked to his cousin Susanna Ingersoll, who lived in an old house in Salem. Her house used to have seven gables. Hawthorne liked the phrase *seven gables.* He didn't have a use for it right away, but he stored it in his writer's memory bank.

Without his Custom House salary, Hawthorne could not stay in Boston. In the spring of 1841, he invested $1,000 in an experimental community called Brook Farm in West Roxbury, Massachusetts, and went there to live. At the farm, agriculture and performing manual labor were supposed to make up the best lifestyle a person could have, enabling one to engage in intellectual pursuits. Each resident would spend a certain amount of time each day performing farm chores, such as hoeing, milking cows, and pitching hay. Then the person would be free to pursue intellectual projects. Hawthorne planned to do his chores for three hours each day, and then spend the rest of his time writing. He hoped that one day he and Sophia would lived there.

He arrived there in a snowstorm on April 12. At first he liked it. He wrote to Louisa that he was becoming a good farmer. Soon, however, he found that his chores were taking much longer than three hours, leaving little time for writing. "My former stories all sprung up of their own accord, out of a quiet life. Now I have no quiet at all,"[1] he complained.

By autumn, Hawthorne had not written anything. In November he left the community.

A new edition of *Twice-Told Tales* appeared at the end of 1841. It contained all the stories from the previous volume, plus some new ones. Although Hawthorne expected to make some money from it, the book did not sell well.

"Surely the book was puffed enough to meet with a sale," Hawthorne said, exasperated. "What the devil is the matter?"[2]

Meanwhile, Sophia finally convinced Hawthorne to tell his family of their engagement. Once he did, Hawthorne and Sophia set a wedding date for June 27, 1842.

As the day approached, Sophia suffered an attack of nerves. The wedding was rescheduled for July 9. On that day, Hawthorne and Sophia were married in the parlor of the Peabody home. She was almost 33 years old and he had just turned 38. None of the Hathornes attended.

"The execution took place yesterday," Hawthorne wrote. "We are as happy as people can be, without making themselves ridiculous. . . ."[3]

The couple rented a home in Concord. Since so many ministers had lived there, Hawthorne called it the Old Manse, a term for a clergy home.

It was a peaceful time. Hawthorne would wander through the orchard in the back of the house, or walk along the nearby Concord River. Sometimes he'd return with an armload of flowers for Sophia. Other times, he'd bring a fish he'd caught for dinner. He planted a garden, and soon they were eating fresh peas and tomatoes. Sometimes the two of them would lie under the trees in each other's arms.

A steady stream of visitors came to Old Manse to see the couple. Margaret Fuller, who considered Hawthorne more of a brother than any man she had ever known, came often.

Another visitor was Henry David Thoreau, a naturalist and writer. He and Hawthorne shared a love of the outdoors. Once in winter the two of them floated down the Concord River on a large piece of ice, towing a boat behind them. Yet Hawthorne did not associate with another local writer, Ralph Waldo Emerson. Throughout their lives, these two giants of American literature never truly understood each other's writing.

Soon Hawthorne realized that in order to support a home and a wife, he needed to make money other than by selling fruit from his orchard. He had written very little since his marriage. Elizabeth Peabody tried to get him a job as the editor of the magazine *Boston Miscellany,* but the position went to someone else (who, showing poor judgment, rejected Edgar Allan Poe's classic horror tale, "The Tell-Tale Heart").

As winter settled in, it seemed to mirror the gloom of Hawthorne's mood. The Old Manse, so airy and comfortable in summer, now seemed chilly and drafty. He hoped for a political appointment to the Salem post office, but did not receive it. He longed to relax next to a roaring fireplace at night, but instead had to settle for sitting next to a hot stove.

Hawthorne tried to write, but found the going slow. He sold some articles and stories to magazines, but was paid very little for them. He hardly had any money for himself, and none to send his family in Salem. What he did write he did not like. The pressure to produce made him tense. "I keep myself uneasy, and produce little, and almost nothing that is worth producing,"[4] he said.

On March 3, 1844, their first child, a daughter, arrived. Sophia named the red-haired girl Una after a character in a poem.

Henry David Thoreau wrote much about nature. His most famous work, Walden, *about the year he spent alone in a cabin in the woods, was published in 1854.*

Una's birth put additional strains on the Hawthornes' thin finances. To keep expenses as low as possible, Nathaniel worked in the kitchen, washing dishes, making breakfast, and doing other chores. He caught fish for dinner and sold fruits and vegetables to supplement their money. When Sophia was away, he went to bed at dusk to save the oil in the lamps. He agreed to a plan to buy up unsold copies of *Twice-Told Tales* so that it could be reissued, but this too failed to make any money.

Hawthorne became convinced that he needed the steady income from a government job. When Democrat James K. Polk was elected president in 1844, Hawthorne's hopes rose for a political appointment. His friends tried to get him a position, but without success.

Finally Hawthorne was offered a job as a clerk at the Charlestown Navy Yard. He rejected it, feeling the job was beneath him.

Every time Hawthorne tried something to make money, it seemed as if bad luck was just waiting to strike. He edited Bridge's travel journal, planning to publish it and keep the profits. As luck would have it, the same month that the journal was published, Frederick Douglass published *Narrative of the Life of Frederick Douglass, An American Slave.* That book became an international sensation, easily eclipsing Bridge's journal.

In October 1845, the Hawthornes had not paid their rent and were evicted from the Old Manse. With nowhere else to go, the struggling writer and his family returned to the Hathorne home in Salem with his mother and sisters. Hawthorne took over his old room under the eaves, and Sophia and the baby took a room on another floor. Hawthorne had never felt lower. He had been forced to return to his mother's house not as a success, but as a penniless writer.

Hawthorne's financial plight was even more acute because Sophia was again pregnant. His political friends kept assuring him that they would get him a job, the but promises did not relieve his worries. "What a devil of a pickle I shall be in," he said, "if the baby should come, and the office should not!"[5]

In March 1846, Hawthorne was appointed surveyor at the Salem Custom House. The salary was $1,200 per year. One of his duties was to check cartons, barrels, and crates to see whether they were correctly labeled. The simple tasks did not take too much effort.

Relieved of financial worries, Hawthorne worked on a new set of stories. On June 5, 1846, they were published as *Mosses from an Old Manse.* Reviews of the work were mostly favorable. However, his friend Margaret Fuller, writing in the *New-York Daily Tribune,* found Hawthorne's style unexciting. Edgar Allan Poe was also mildly critical. Wiley and Putnam, the book's publishers, went bankrupt shortly after its publication.

Chapter **4**   DESPERATION AND TRIUMPH

Later that month, on June 22, Sophia gave birth to a boy, Julian. Hawthorne jokingly called him the Black Prince because of his dark curly hair and red cheeks. A little over a year later, Hawthorne and his family moved to a new home at 14 Mall Street in Salem. They still didn't have much money, but it was at least a home of their own again. Hawthorne set up in a quiet third-floor study and began writing more regularly.

In the 1848 election, Zachary Taylor won over his Democratic opponent, putting the Whigs back in power. Hawthorne knew what that meant. Although he tried hard to save his job, he was fired on June 8, 1849.

The following month, his mother died. It was one of the most depressing times ever for Hawthorne: no job, no income, and now no mother. He received some overdue money from friends; others sent him money because his writing had elevated American literature. Sophia helped out when she could, using her artistic skills to decorate lampshades and books. Still, it was not enough.

At this dark time, a light appeared in the form of an editor named James T. Fields. He visited the author in the fall of 1849 to find out what Hawthorne had been writing. Fields and his partners, William Davis Ticknor and John Reed, owned perhaps the most prestigious book publishing firm in America: Ticknor, Reed, and Fields of Boston.

According to Fields, he repeatedly asked Hawthorne what he had been writing. Nothing, Hawthorne kept replying gloomily. Fields gave up and began walking down some stairs to leave the house. Before he reached the last step, however, Hawthorne was behind him, pushing a large manuscript into his hands. It was either very good or very bad, Hawthorne said; he didn't know which. Fields read the story on the train back to Boston and decided it was very, very good. He immediately returned to Salem, knowing that the story was destined to be a literary classic. That story ultimately became *The Scarlet Letter.*

Every writer needs a good editor, and now Hawthorne had found one. Sensing the awesome power of the work, Fields suggested that it be printed by itself, instead of grouped with other stories. The two compromised: a short piece called "The Custom House," although it had no relation to it, would open the book containing *The Scarlet Letter.*

On March 16, 1850, two thousand five hundred copies of *The Scarlet Letter* were printed. They sold out in two weeks. A second edition of 1,500 copies sold out in three days. Reviewers praised the book, calling Hawthorne one of the giants of literature. After years of struggle, heartbreak, and financial turmoil, he had finally made it as a writer.

He decided to leave Salem. It held only bad memories for him, and now with his mother dead there was little reason to stay. He rented a house in Lenox, Massachusetts, in the Berkshire Mountains. Its rooms were small, but it had a beautiful lake behind it, and gorgeous hills and mountains as its background.

On August 5, 1850, a young writer named Herman Melville came to the Hawthornes' for a picnic. Melville was a former sailor who had lived the type of adventurous life on the high seas that Hawthorne had always dreamed about. He wrote a glowing review of Hawthorne's *Mosses from an Old Manse.* Melville liked Hawthorne so much that he dedicated his next book—a novel about whaling, the cost of revenge, and much more, called *Moby-Dick*—to Hawthorne.

With the success of *The Scarlet Letter,* Hawthorne felt a new type of pressure: the pressure to produce another book equally as good. Fields urged him to write more. He was already reissuing the books published by Peabody. He also planned yet another edition of *Twice-Told Tales,* and was busy with other Hawthorne projects. Yet he knew that a new novel by the writer of *The Scarlet Letter* would probably sell best of all.

In the fall of 1850, Hawthorne began to write. He told Fields that the new book would not be ready before January. He wanted to make the book lighter in tone than the very grim and moody *Scarlet Letter* because he was becoming concerned by his reputation for "gloomy" writing. (He once told Elizabeth Peabody that he had burned some stories because he thought they were too dark and depressing.) He also found that the new book required more effort than *The Scarlet Letter.*

"I find the book requires more care and thought than *The Scarlet Letter;* also, I have to wait oftener for a mood,"[6] he said to Fields.

When the new book was finally finished, Hawthorne called it *The House of the Seven Gables,* retrieving from his memory the images and stories of Susanna Ingersoll's house. The background for *The House of*

Herman Melville dedicated his most famous work Moby Dick, *to Nathaniel Hawthorne.*

the Seven Gables was the infamous Salem Witch Trials, and his belief that the misdeeds of one generation live on to stain successive ones.

Published in April 1851, the new book received mainly good reviews. Most reviewers liked it; a few claimed that the first hundred pages were brilliant, but thereafter the book was weak. Perhaps the reading public agreed, because sales were slower than expected.

On May 20, 1851, just after *Seven Gables* was published, Sophia gave birth to daughter Rose. The next year Hawthorne wrote a children's book that retold classic myths called *A Wonder Book for Girls and Boys*.

The addition of another child made the small house in Lenox even smaller. Worried anew about money, Hawthorne retreated once again to a life of seclusion. He was rarely seen in the village, except to visit the post office. Around Melville, the former sailor still full of sea stories, Hawthorne grew even more restless for the ocean. He told Sophia that he hated the area and would gladly see the Berkshire Mountains flattened.

Although the election of 1852 was still far off, Hawthorne wanted to be close to Boston. He felt the Democratic Party had a good chance of retaking the White House, and he wanted to be near a major city, where the people were who could offer him a job if the Democrats won.

In November 1851, the Hawthorne family left Lenox. They moved to West Newton, a twenty-minute train ride from Boston. In December, Fields republished stories that had appeared in *The Token* as *The Snow-Image, and Other Twice-Told Tales*. With Fields pressuring him and a new baby to care for, Hawthorne locked himself in his study and wrote eight hours or more per day. The resulting book, which was based on his Brook Farm experiences and entitled *The Blithedale Romance,* was a critical and commercial failure. "Let us hope there are no more Blithedales,"[7] grumbled Fields, comparing the book's poor sales to those of Harriet Beecher Stowe's extremely popular *Uncle Tom's Cabin*.

In May 1852, the Hawthornes moved again. This time they bought a home in Concord. It was the first house Hawthorne had ever owned. He called it The Wayside.

That summer, Hawthorne's friend Franklin Pierce ran for the presidency. Hawthorne hurried to Boston and offered to write a campaign biography of Pierce. He had barely begun the project when tragedy struck: his sister Louisa was a passenger on a steamboat that had been racing another boat on the Hudson River. Louisa's ship careened out of control, and frightened passengers jumped into the water, hoping to swim to safety. Some, including Louisa, drowned. Hawthorne took the news hard.

Hawthorne purchased The Wayside from Bronson Alcott, whose daughter Louisa May would write the classic novel Little Women. *The story would take place in this very house.*

When he finally finished his biography of Pierce, it angered many people, especially in New England. The region was a hotbed of the antislavery movement. They detested Pierce because they considered him too sympathetic to the proslavery South. Even so, Pierce was elected the fourteenth president of the United States. Hawthorne was closer than ever to the government post he had always dreamed about.

FYInfo

The Scarlet Letter

The Scarlet Letter cemented Hawthorne's reputation as a great writer. What makes *The Scarlet Letter* such a classic of literature?

When the book was written, the American literary scene was just coming into its own. Americans were eager to read American writers writing about American topics. Hawthorne's book, about the historical Puritans, was timely. It was the novel that announced America's literary scene to be the equal of any in the world.

But there was more to it than that. At the core of the book is the complex predicament that women face as wives, mothers, daughters, and sexual beings. Hester Prynne, the main character, is trying to gain an understanding of herself throughout the book. It is one of the first books to deal with a woman's role in society. Some call it the first American psychological novel.

The book also deals with subjects that American books had not done before, such as adultery and passion. The story takes place in colonial Boston. Prynne has

Demi Moore playing Hester Prynne

committed adultery, and according to the dictates of society, must wear a scarlet letter *A* so that all will know of her immorality. Although subjected to severe pressure, she refuses to name the man with whom she had an affair—the father of her child. The book shows just how destructive the use of public shame, guilt, and revenge can be. In *The Scarlet Letter*, Hawthorne is comparing the Puritans' very strict morality with the feelings of passion and emotion that are within every person.

Hawthorne around 1860. He had just returned to America after living abroad. The author, having finally achieved artistic and financial success, was much more at peace with himself.

Chapter 5

LIVING ABROAD

Pierce rewarded his friend with a choice political job. On March 26, 1853, the U.S. Senate approved Hawthorne as the American Consul to England. He hurriedly finished *Tanglewood Tales,* a sequel to *A Wonder Book for Girls and Boys,* and prepared to leave for England.

Some biographers question why Hawthorne accepted the job when he had finally achieved the literary recognition that he had longed for all his life. Why trade that in for a government job?

The answer may be that although he had become known among the reading public, Hawthorne always worried about money and wanted to earn a steady income for his family. In addition, because he was well known, he had to continue producing stories, books, and articles. Hawthorne was not that type of writer: He worked best when the pressure was off, when he did not have to write. With the consulship, the pressure was indeed off, but Hawthorne would find other reasons not to write. It would be seven years until he published anything again.

On July 6, 1853, the Hawthornes left America for Liverpool, England. The family did not like Great Britain.

It rained often, Liverpool was dirty and dingy, and the children became homesick. Hawthorne in particular did not relish his duties. These included investigating complaints about conditions aboard American ships, interpreting maritime law, and providing passage home to American sailors who had gotten stranded in England. If it weren't for the money, Hawthorne said, he'd resign. He found himself missing something that he'd never thought he'd miss—writing.

Hawthorne filled notebooks with impressions of England and its people. He noted the differences between the lives of people struggling to survive on the street and those of people who were wealthy.

Sophia also grew to detest England—and Hawthorne's job as consul. She disliked the long hours of separation when Hawthorne was at his office. She had become used to having him around often, even if he was locked in his study writing. The poor weather, depressing city, and Hawthorne's duties combined to cause problems in their marriage.

In the spring of 1855, Sophia developed a hacking cough. She claimed it was the same type of cough that had killed her mother. She refused to go outside and breathe the moist air. In October, concerned about her health with winter's dampness coming on, Hawthorne sent her to sunny Portugal with Una and Rose. It was the first lengthy separation of their marriage. Little wonder that he wailed, "I HATE England."[1]

Even so, he did not quit his job and return to writing. One reason was the explosion of new writers in America. Each was a threat to the territory and readership he had staked out. In addition, the runaway success of Harriet Beecher Stowe's *Uncle Tom's Cabin* had brought many women into the literary world—a situation Hawthorne truly detested. "All women, as authors, are feeble and tiresome," he raged. "I wish they were forbidden to write."[2] To him, writers did their best work when they appeared before the public with no pretensions—in effect, hiding no secrets. A proper woman, thought Hawthorne, always had secrets. Sophia agreed with him. When Una began writing stories and expressed interest in a writing career, Sophia ignored her.

After nearly nine months away, Sophia returned to England on June 9, 1856, still coughing. The family did not want to go back to Liverpool, so they began wandering all over the English countryside, trying to find a suitable home, while Hawthorne commuted to Liverpool. They tried Blackheath, Southport, Old Trafford, and Bath, without success. England was clearly not for them.

The Hawthornes would have returned to America, but the country was on the verge of civil war. Hawthorne read with dismay the newspaper accounts of the lawlessness and violence sweeping over the United States and of the increasingly bitter disputes between the pro- and antislavery forces. He told Bridge that it sickened him to look back at America. Unlike many other New Englanders, he was not a fierce slavery opponent.

James Buchanan was elected president in the election of 1856. This brought Hawthorne's political career to an end. Although Buchanan was also a Democrat, he would want to appoint his own man to the consul's job. So on February 13, 1857, Hawthorne resigned the post, effective six months later on the final day of August. After several delays, the Hawthornes finally left England on January 5, 1858.

They did not return to America. Instead the family went to Paris, France. Initially Hawthorne loved the French city, but soon he was complaining about the biting cold and the narrow fireplaces at their hotel. On March 20, the Hawthornes arrived in Rome, Italy.

Rome, a city Sophia had always wanted to visit, did wonders for her health. Her cough and headaches vanished, and she was soon roaming about the city. Hawthorne accompanied her with far less enthusiasm. Rome, he said, was like a decaying corpse.

However, he was fascinated by a sculpture called *Resting Satyr (Standing Faun)*. The faun was a mythical humanlike creature. The sculpture showed a humanlike youth, leaning on a tree limb with a sly smile playing about his lips. Intrigued by the sculpture, Hawthorne returned to see it again. His lively imagination, unused for so long, would remember this image.

When the Hawthornes left Rome, they headed for Florence, Italy. Hawthorne, his good mood slowly returning, was beginning to write again. He told Fields that he was planning two romances.

The Hawthornes returned to Rome on October 1, 1858. They had barely gotten settled in when Una came down with a severe case of malaria. Over the next few months, her condition kept changing between seriously ill and recovering. Hawthorne tried to write for an hour or two each day, but he had always been able to write only when there was nothing else on his mind. Una's illness, and the constant interruptions informing him of some new medical crisis or change in her condition, made him uncertain of his work's quality. "I have had too many interruptions . . . the story has developed itself in a very imperfect way,"[3] he told Fields. Then he too became ill, possibly also with malaria. This was the first major illness that he had ever contracted.

While he got better, Una seemed to be sinking. She announced to her mother in March that she was going to die. In early April the doctor agreed, telling Sophia that Una might not live through the night.

Friends in Rome rushed to the Hawthornes to comfort them. Most notable was Franklin Pierce, who was vacationing in Rome with his wife. At least once a day, he visited the Hawthornes and forced the anxious author to walk with him outside to try to relieve some of his stress. A grateful Sophia said that Hawthorne kept his sanity during this dark period only because of Pierce.

Eventually Una began to recover. Her doctor insisted that she remain in Rome during her recuperation, but Hawthorne could not bear to stay in the city. On June 23, 1859, the family arrived once again in Great Britain. Fields had sold Hawthorne's new book to a British firm, and Hawthorne had to stay in England to revise the book and get it ready for printing.

He finished his new book in November. Entitled *Transformation* in England and *The Marble Faun* in America (with a subtitle of *The Romance of Monte Beni* for both editions), the book drew upon Hawthorne's experiences in Rome, his despair over Una's illness, and his feelings of growing old. It was a critical and commercial success, and is today considered one of his best. Just one month after its English publication, the book entered a third printing.

The Hawthornes returned to The Wayside in June 1860. Although happy to be home, Hawthorne was concerned about the uproar over the slavery issue.

It had been seven years since he had last lived in America. Both he and the country were much changed. The shadow of civil war hung heavy in the air, as neighbor prepared to fight neighbor.

The Civil War battle at Fort Donelson, Tennessee, gave the Union an important victory on February 16, 1862.

Hawthorne attended meetings of the Saturday Club, a social group for writers. There he usually ate quickly, kept his eyes downcast, and did not talk much. He was still a loner. He had a small tower added to The Wayside, and there he would escape for hours at a time.

He tried to write, but he produced little besides a few magazine articles. He blamed his lack of productivity on the Civil War, which had started in April 1861.

In July 1862, Hawthorne produced a defiantly antiwar essay called "Chiefly About War Matters by a Peaceable Man." A year later, he published *Our Old Home: A Series of English Sketches,* based on his experiences as consul. He dedicated the book to Franklin Pierce.

Hawthorne tried writing a new novel and Fields announced in the pages of a magazine that a new work by Hawthorne would soon appear.

Chapter **5**   LIVING ABROAD

But there would be no new book. Hawthorne's powers of concentration were fading, and so was his physical strength. He tried dragging logs down from the top of a hill to the bottom to recover his strength, but it was no use. The man who never got sick was now gravely ill. He worried about money and about growing old. Newspapers, with grim war news and long lists of casualties, depressed him. Death seemed everywhere. "I do not know what I shall do with him,"[4] Sophia worried.

No one knew what to do with him, for no one knew what was wrong with him. His body was shrinking, his stomach constantly hurt, his vision was blurry, his hands trembled, and his strength was fading. When Emerson came to visit him in March 1864, Hawthorne was too weak to even pull on his boots.

Before that, with a touch of his old sarcasm, he told Fields to announce his retirement to the public. Hawthorne joked that Fields should say, "Mr. Hawthorne's brain is addled at last. . . ."[5]

Ticknor decided that a trip to warmer climates would do Hawthorne good. In Philadelphia, he gave the feeble Hawthorne his overcoat to protect him from a cold rain. But then Ticknor caught a cold that turned into pneumonia. On April 10, 1864, Ticknor died in a Philadelphia hotel. A friend found Hawthorne wandering the hotel halls in a daze, convinced that Death had taken the wrong man.

However, less than two weeks later, Hawthorne was ready for another trip. This time his traveling companion would be Franklin Pierce.

Meeting in Boston, the two men traveled to New Hampshire. On May 18, they arrived in Plymouth. Hawthorne had become so weak that he had to be lifted out of the carriage in which he was traveling. According to legend, Hawthorne and Pierce spent that night drinking. In actuality, Hawthorne had a cup of tea and toast. He then went to bed. That is where Pierce found him dead the next morning. Nathaniel Hawthorne was fifty-nine years old.

Hawthorne once wrote, "Men die, finally, because they choose not the toil and torment of struggling longer with Time, for mere handsfull of moments."[6] For this unique man, who overcame numerous obstacles to become one of the greatest American writers, the struggle was over.

FYInfo

Franklin Pierce

Franklin Pierce

Franklin Pierce was a true "dark horse" (someone about whom little is known) candidate for the presidency. A Bowdoin College schoolmate of Hawthorne's, Pierce was nominated by the Democratic Party at their presidential convention in 1852 after it was hopelessly deadlocked. Forty-eight ballots had not produced a candidate acceptable to both the antislavery northern Democrats and the proslavery southern Democrats. On the forty-ninth ballot, Pierce, a Senator from New Hampshire who had proslavery views, was unexpectedly put forth as a candidate and won the nomination. In the general election, he won a narrow victory over the Whig Party candidate, General Winfield Scott.

Despite Hawthorne's prediction that his old classmate could be a great leader, Pierce's presidency was a disaster. He continually agreed with the views of southern congressmen, angering the antislavery North. Perhaps his worst decision was to support slavery in the new territory of Kansas. This touched off a bloody struggle in Kansas between pro- and antislavery forces. The fighting was so intense and violent that the state became known as Bleeding Kansas. It was during this time that John Brown, whom many credit for hastening the beginning of the Civil War, became a national figure by participating in the slavery battle.

Pierce also did some good, however, such as authorizing James Gadsden to peacefully purchase land that became southern Arizona and New Mexico. But in the America of the 1850s, slavery was the overriding issue, and here he failed miserably. He later became a bitter opponent of Abraham Lincoln and the Civil War. He died in 1869.

CHRONOLOGY

1804	Nathaniel Hathorne born on July 4 in Salem, Massachusetts
1808	Father, Captain Nathaniel Hathorne, dies
1813	Grandfather Manning dies; is temporarily crippled by foot injury
1825	Graduates from Bowdoin College
1828	Publishes *Fanshawe*
1836	Edits *American Magazine of Useful and Entertaining Knowledge*
1839	Appointed to Boston Custom House (to 1840); becomes engaged to Sophia Peabody
1841	Lives at Brook Farm Commune in West Roxbury, Massachusetts
1842	Marries Sophia Peabody on July 9
1844	Daughter Una born on March 3
1846	Son Julian born on June 22; appointed Surveyor of the Port of Salem at Salem Custom House (to 1849)
1849	Mother, Elizabeth Clarke Manning Hathorne, dies; meets editor James T. Fields
1850	Publishes *The Scarlet Letter;* family moves to Lenox; meets Herman Melville
1851	Publishes *The House of the Seven Gables;* daughter Rose born on May 20; rents home in West Newton
1852	Buys house, The Wayside, in Concord; sister Louisa drowns
1853–57	Serves as United States Consul at Liverpool, England
1857–60	Lives in France, Italy, and England
1860	Returns to America; publishes *The Marble Faun*
1864	Dies in Plymouth, New Hampshire, on May 19

SELECTED WORKS

1837, 1841, 1851	*Twice-Told Tales*
1841	*The Whole History of Grandfather's Chair*
1846, 1854	*Mosses from an Old Manse*
1850	*The Scarlet Letter*
1851	*The House of the Seven Gables*
1852	*A Wonder Book for Girls and Boys*
1852	*The Blithedale Romance*
	The Life of Franklin Pierce
	The Snow-Image, and Other Twice-Told Tales
1853	*Tanglewood Tales*
1860	*The Marble Faun; Or, the Romance of Monte Beni*
1862	"Chiefly About War Matters by a Peaceable Man"
1863	*Our Old Home: A Series of English Sketches*

TIMELINE IN HISTORY

1792 First edition of *The Farmer's Almanac* appears.

1794 Eli Whitney patents the cotton gin.

1800 Johnny Appleseed begins traveling west; first pair of shoes made with specific left and right.

1804 Aaron Burr shoots Alexander Hamilton in a duel.

1805 Lewis & Clark reach the Pacific Ocean.

1807 *The Clermont*, the world's first serviceable steamboat, makes its maiden voyage.

1811 An earthquake in Missouri makes the Mississippi River run backward.

1814 Francis Scott Key writes "The Star-Spangled Banner."

1820 Washington Irving publishes "The Legend of Sleepy Hollow" and "Rip Van Winkle."

1826 The first American steam locomotive is demonstrated in Hoboken, New Jersey.

1827 John James Audubon publishes *The Birds of America*.

1829 The Tremont Hotel, the first modern U.S. hotel, opens in Boston.

1836 Mexican troops storm the Alamo.

1839 Charles Goodyear accidentally discovers vulcanization, a process for making rubber.

1841 Edgar Allan Poe publishes "The Murders in the Rue Morgue."

1845 Alexander Cartwright helps establish the modern rules of baseball.

1846 Elias Howe patents the sewing machine.

1848 James Marshall discovers gold in California.

1851 Herman Melville publishes *Moby-Dick;* Emanuel Leutze paints *Washington Crossing the Delaware*.

1853 Gail Borden invents condensed milk.

1855 Walt Whitman publishes *Leaves of Grass*.

1857 Nathaniel Currier and James Merritt Ives begin making hand-colored prints.

1859 Oil is discovered in Pennsylvania.

1861 The American Civil War begins.

1863 Thanksgiving Day is declared a national holiday.

1869 Rutgers beats Princeton in the first college football game.

1871 The Great Chicago Fire kills 300 people.

1876 The telephone is patented.

1879 Thomas Edison discovers a filament material for his electric lightbulb.

1881 Billy the Kid is killed in New Mexico.

1886 The Statue of Liberty is dedicated.

1900 L. Frank Baum publishes his *Oz* series, the story of *The Wonderful Wizard of Oz*.

1903 Binney & Smith introduce Crayola crayons.

1908 Henry Ford introduces the Model T automobile.

CHAPTER NOTES

Chapter Two   The Boy Who Wanted to Be a Writer

1. Mark Van Doren, *Nathaniel Hawthorne* (New York: William Sloane Associates, 1949), p. 11.

2. Brenda Wineapple, *Hawthorne, A Life* (New York: Alfred A. Knopf, 2003), p. 39.

3. Ibid, p. 42.

4. Ibid, p. 54.

Chapter Three   A New Name and a New Love

1. Brenda Wineapple, *Hawthorne, A Life* (New York: Alfred A. Knopf, 2003), p. 63.

2. Mark Van Doren, *Nathaniel Hawthorne* (New York: William Sloane Associates, 1949), p. 26.

3. Edward Wagenknecht, *Nathaniel Hawthorne: Man and Writer* (New York: Oxford University Press, 1961), p. 20.

4. Wineapple, p. 90.

5. Wagenknecht, p. 76.

6. Wineapple, p. 134.

Chapter Four   Desperation and Triumph

1. Brenda Wineapple, *Hawthorne, A Life* (New York: Alfred A. Knopf, 2003), p. 150.

2. Ibid., p. 155.

3. Edward Wagenknecht, *Nathaniel Hawthorne: Man and Writer* (New York: Oxford University Press, 1961), p. 99.

4. Wineapple, p. 174.

5. Ibid., p. 192.

6. Mark Van Doren, *Nathaniel Hawthorne* (New York: William Sloane Associates, 1949), p. 171.

7. Wineapple, p. 255.

Chapter Five   Living Abroad

1. Brenda Wineapple, *Hawthorne, A Life* (New York: Alfred A. Knopf, 2003), p. 275.

2. Edward Wagenknecht, *Nathaniel Hawthorne: Man and Writer* (New York: Oxford University Press, 1961), p. 150.

3. Wineapple, p. 313.

4. Ibid., p. 367.

5. Wagenknecht, p. 99.

6. Wineapple, p. 373.

FURTHER READING

For Young Adults

Hawthorne, Hildegarde. *Romantic Rebel: The Story of Nathaniel Hawthorne.* New York: Appleton-Century-Crofts, 1960.

Morey, Eileen. *Readings on "The Scarlet Letter."* San Diego: Greenhaven Press, 1998.

Swisher, Clarice. *The Scarlet Letter.* Understanding Great Literature. San Diego: Lucent Books, 2003.

Whitelaw, Nancy. *Nathaniel Hawthorne: American Storyteller.* Greensboro, North Carolina: Morgan Reynolds, Inc., 1996.

Wood, James Playsted. *The Unpardonable Sin: A Life of Nathaniel Hawthorne.* New York: Pantheon Books, 1970.

Works Consulted

Hoeltje, Hubert. *Inward Sky: The Mind and Heart of Nathaniel Hawthorne.* Durham, North Carolina: Duke University Press, 1962.

Van Doren, Mark. *Nathaniel Hawthorne.* New York: William Sloane Associates, 1949.

Wagenknecht, Edward. *Nathaniel Hawthorne: The Man, His Tales and Romances.* New York: The Continuum Publishing Company, 1989.

———. *Nathaniel Hawthorne: Man and Writer.* New York: Oxford University Press, 1961.

Wineapple, Brenda. *Hawthorne, A Life.* New York: Alfred A. Knopf, 2003.

On the Internet

Nathaniel Hawthorne (1804–1864) Home Page from Eldritch Press
http://www.eldritchpress.org/nh/hawthorne.html

Nathaniel Hawthorne in Salem
http://www.hawthorneinsalem.org/

Nathaniel Hawthorne—Biography and Works
http://www.online-literature.com/hawthorne

Nathaniel Hawthorne—*The Scarlet Letter;* The Classic Text: Traditions and Interpretations
http://www.uwm.edu/Libraries/special/exhibits/clastext/clspg143.htm

O'Toole, Heather: "The Blackness of Men's Souls: Why Nathaniel Hawthorne Could Not Embrace Transcendentalism"
http://www.bridgewater.edu/philo/philo96/otoole.html

The Wayside: Home of Authors
http://www.nps.gov/mima/wayside/index1.htm

INDEX